Viola Time Sprinters

a third book of pieces for viola

Kathy and David Blackwell

T0057075

Welcome to ***Viola Time Sprinters***. You'll find:

- pieces using the finger pattern 01–2–34, plus low 2nd fingers and high 3rd fingers
- 2nd and 3rd position pieces
- a range of bowing techniques, including spiccato, hooked bowing, and string crossing
- original pieces in different styles plus well-known pieces
- pieces using modes, the chromatic and blues scales, and dominant 7ths
- duets with parts of equal difficulty
- CD of performances and backings, with drumkit and bass added for the jazz and rock numbers
- piano and viola accompaniments available separately.

Pieces with piano accompaniment are presented in two formats on the CD: firstly, a complete performance, then the accompaniment only, which you can play along to. There is a count-in when the viola and piano parts start together.

This symbol is placed alongside all the pieces that appear on the accompanying CD. When there are two numbers given in the symbol, the top number indicates the complete performance, and the bottom number the accompaniment alone.

In all duet pieces, the top part is assigned to the right-hand channel and the lower part to the left-hand channel. You can choose to play along with either part by muting the appropriate channel.

MUSIC DEPARTMENT

OXFORD
UNIVERSITY PRESS

OXFORD
UNIVERSITY PRESS

Great Clarendon Street, Oxford OX2 6DP, England

Oxford University Press is a department of the University of Oxford.
It furthers the University's aim of excellence in research, scholarship,
and education by publishing worldwide

Oxford is a registered trade mark of Oxford University Press
in the UK and in certain other countries

This collection © Oxford University Press 2008

Kathy and David Blackwell have asserted their right under the Copyright, Designs
and Patents Act, 1988, to be identified as the Composers of this Work.

Database right Oxford University Press (maker)

First published 2008. Reprinted with corrections 2013.

All rights reserved. No part of this publication may be reproduced,
stored in a retrieval system, or transmitted, in any form or by any means,
without the prior permission in writing of Oxford University Press,
or as expressly permitted by law. Enquiries concerning reproduction
outside the scope of the above should be sent to the Music Copyright
Department, Oxford University Press, at the address above

Permission to perform the works in this anthology in public
(except in the course of divine worship) should normally be obtained
from the Performing Right Society Ltd. (PRS), 29/33 Berners Street,
London W1T 3AB, or its affiliated Societies in each country throughout
the world, unless the owner or the occupier of the premises
being used holds a licence from the Society

Permission to make a recording must be obtained in advance
from the Mechanical Copyright Protection Society Ltd. (MCPS),
Elgar House, 41 Streatham High Road, London SW16 1ER,
or its affiliated Societies in each country throughout the world

17

ISBN 978–0–19–336081–5

Music and text origination by
Barnes Music Engraving Ltd., East Sussex

Printed in Great Britain on acid-free paper by
Halstan & Co. Ltd., Amersham, Bucks.

Unless otherwise marked, all pieces are by Kathy and David Blackwell
and are © Oxford University Press. All traditional pieces,
and nos. 3, 11, 19, 20, 25, and 35, are arranged by Kathy and
David Blackwell and are © Oxford University Press. Unauthorized
arrangement or photocopying of this copyright material is ILLEGAL.

Contents

1. Ready to rock 4
2. Clear skies 4
3. Ode to joy (Beethoven) (*duet*) 5
4. Song from the show 6
5. Starry night 6
6. Paris café 7
7. Gaudete! (*duet*) 8
8. Jacob's dance 9
9. Sprint finish 9
10. Bolero (*duet*) 10
11. William Tell (Rossini) 11
12. Country gardens (*duet*) 12
13. You and me (*duet*) 13
14. The road to Donegal 14
15. Full circle (*duet*) 15
16. Thirsty work 16
17. Farewell to Skye 17
18. Lady Katherine's pavane 17
19. Dance of the Sugar Plum Fairy (Tchaikovsky) 18
20. Allegro in D (Telemann) 18
21. Still reeling 19
22. Mexican fiesta 20
23. Show stopper 20
24. Spy movie 21
25. Largo, from the *New World* Symphony (Dvořák) (*duet*) 22
26. Hornpipe, from the *Water Music* (Handel) 23
27. Hungarian folk dance 24
28. Wild West 25
29. Midnight song 26
30. Wade in the water 27
31. Dominant gene (*duet*) 28
32. Chromatic cats 29
33. Show off! 29
34. Little lamb 30
35. Habanera, from *Carmen* (Bizet) 31
36. Alleluia (Boyce) 32
37. Jubilate Deo (Mozart) 32
38. Round Trinidad Bay 32

1 2
1. Ready to rock
KB & DB
Determined
f
5
9
ff
13
mp
cresc.
ff

3 4
2. Clear skies
KB & DB
Relaxed
2
mp
7
11
cresc.
15
rit.
mp
p

3. *Ode to joy*

(from Symphony No. 9)

Ludwig van Beethoven (1770–1827)

Also try this in 3rd position using the fingering given.

4. Song from the show

KB & DB

5. Starry night

KB & DB

6. *Paris café*

10 ○ 11

KB & DB

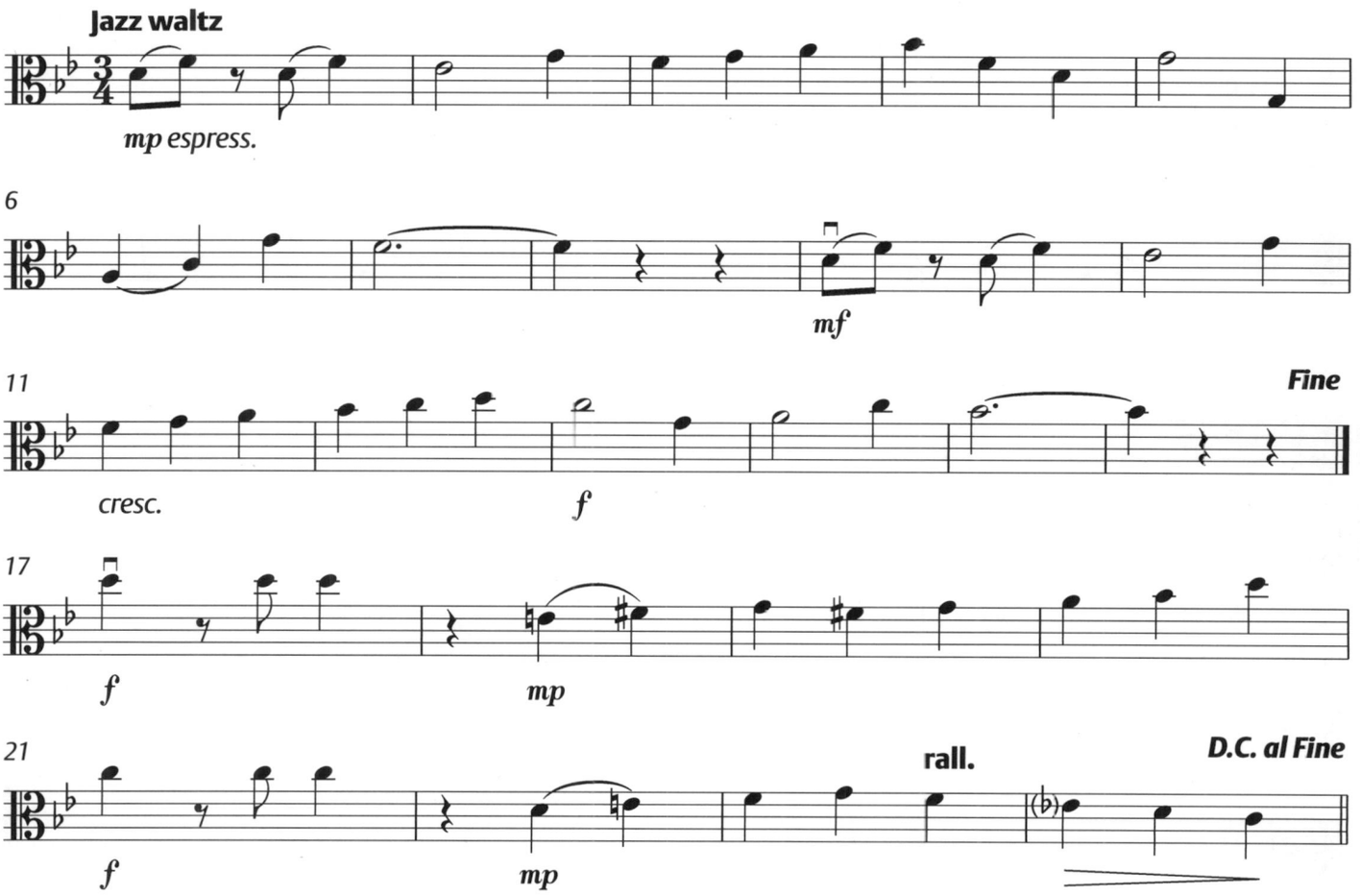

7. Gaudete!

Medieval carol

8. *Jacob's dance*

13 ○ 14

KB & DB

9. *Sprint finish*

15 ○ 16

KB & DB

10. Bolero

L 17 ○ 18 R

Spanish trad.

This piece can be played as a solo or duet with piano, or as an unaccompanied viola duet.

11. *William Tell*

G. A. Rossini (1792–1868)

Warm up

Repeat an octave higher.

12. Country gardens

English Morris Dance tune

13. You and me

L 22 R

KB & DB

14. The road to Donegal

KB & DB

Warm up

etc.

Try a C major scale/arpeggio with hooked bowing.

15. Full circle

16. *Thirsty work*

26 ○ 27

KB & DB

Variation: the chorus and verse 1 can be played in semiquavers with spiccato bowing, as demonstrated in the final chorus on the CD.

Warm ups

Repeat on the D and A strings.

17. *Farewell to Skye*

28 ○ 29

KB & DB

18. *Lady Katherine's pavane*

30 ○ 31

KB & DB

The pavane was a slow, stately court dance popular in the 16th and 17th centuries.

32 ○ 33

19. *Dance of the Sugar Plum Fairy*

(from the *Nutcracker* ballet)

P. I. Tchaikovsky (1840–93)

Andante

p sempre stacc.

5

mf

9

p

13

f

34 ○ 35

20. *Allegro in D*

G. P. Telemann (1681–1767)

Allegro

f (p)

5

mp

9

cresc.

mf

13

f

Try starting this piece with either a down or an up bow.

21. *Still reeling*

(based on *Blair Atholl*, trad. Scottish reel)

Add your own dynamics to this reel.

A second player could add a drone accompaniment using these two chords; how about a drum/bodran rhythm too?

22. *Mexican fiesta*

38 ○ 39

KB & DB

Use these words to help with the rhythm:

23. *Show stopper*

40 ○ 41

KB & DB

42 ○ 43

24. Spy movie

KB & DB

Creepy

25. *Largo*

(from the *New World* Symphony)

Antonín Dvořák (1841–1904)

26. *Hornpipe*

(from the *Water Music*)

G. F. Handel (1685–1759)

27. Hungarian folk dance

KB & DB

Lively

mp staccato

7

f

12

p

17

f

mp

24

f

30

37

(2nd time **accelerando**)

mf (*ff*)

43

1.

2.

ff

Warm ups

Try these two warm ups in the Lydian mode.

stacc.

stacc.

28. *Wild West*

49 ○ 50

KB & DB

Warm up

Use this warm up to practise changing quickly from 1st to 3rd position.

29. *Midnight song*

KB & DB

Warm up

Practise legato shifts from 1st to 3rd position with this warm up.

Also try on the G and A strings.

30. *Wade in the water*

Spiritual

Warm ups

Sing and play this warm up a few times to get the feel of the syncopated rhythm.

Wade_____ in the wa - ter,___

Play the blues scale on G.

Play this rhythm on each note of the blues scale on G.

31. Dominant gene

32. Chromatic cats

56 ○ 57

KB & DB

33. Show off!

58 ○ 59

KB & DB

34. *Little lamb*

Spiritual

Light and graceful

mp (stay in 2nd position)

6

10

f *mp* *f*

14

mp

18

22

26

rall.

mp *dim.* *p*

Warm ups

Play an F major scale in 2nd position like this:

etc.

Lit - tle lamb, oh lit - tle lamb, oh

35. *Habanera*

(from *Carmen*)

Georges Bizet (1838–75)

Warm up

To get the feel of the triplet rhythm, try playing a chromatic scale on G with this pattern:

Round up

Play these rounds or canons in 2 or more parts, entering at *.

64

36. Alleluia

William Boyce (1711–79)

65

37. Jubilate Deo

W. A. Mozart (1756–91)

66

38. Round Trinidad Bay

KB & DB